Children with Enemies

PHOENIX POETS

STUART DISCHELL

Children with Enemies

THE UNIVERSITY OF CHICAGO PRESS

Chicago & London

The University of Chicago Press, Chicago 60637
The University of Chicago Press, Ltd., London
© 2017 by The University of Chicago
Published 2017
Printed in the United States of America

26 25 24 23 22 21 20 19 18 17   1 2 3 4 5

ISBN-13: 978-0-226-49859-1 (paper)
ISBN-13: 978-0-226-49862-1 (e-book)
DOI: 10.7208/chicago/9780226498621.001.0001

Library of Congress Cataloging-in-Publication Data

Names: Dischell, Stuart, author.
Title: Children with enemies / Stuart Dischell.
Other titles: Phoenix poets.
Description: Chicago : The University of Chicago Press, 2017. |
    Series: Phoenix poets
Identifiers: LCCN 2016059827 | ISBN 9780226498591 (pbk. : alk. paper) |
    ISBN 9780226498621 (e-book)
Classification: LCC PS3554.I827 C48 2017 | DDC 811/.54—dc23 LC record
    available at https://lccn.loc.gov/2016059827

♾ This paper meets the requirements of ANSI/NISO Z39.48-1992
(Permanence of Paper).

For Tara

Unhappy is the land that needs a hero.

Bertolt Brecht, *Galileo*

CONTENTS

ACKNOWLEDGMENTS

Some of these poems first appeared, sometimes in different versions or under other titles, in the following publications:

Agni: "Evening in the Window, Parts I–IV," "Questions for the Mariner," and "Translation from the Origins of Time"

Asheville Poetry Review: "Casualty Event" and "Why Poseidon Chose My Grandfather"

Barnstorm: "Without Sunglasses"

Birmingham Poetry Review: "Another Picture of the Future"

Cerise Press: "The Mysteries of Aurora"

Cortland Review: "Because You Have Seen It So," "In the Sequences of Traffic," "On the Day after My Birthday," and "Things Are Changing for Johanna"

Eleven Eleven: "Others Made It Over the Pyrenees"

Five Points: "Ring of Keys" and "The Best for Me"

Forklift, Ohio: "Little Narcissus" and "My Famous Broken Heart"

Gulf Coast: a version of section VI of "The Mysteries of Aurora"

New South: "Future Girl"

Northwest Review: "What Begins in Eros Ends in Elegy" and "Okay to Others"

One: "A Visit to a Strange Land"

Ploughshares: "The Lives of My Friends"

Sliver of Stone: "Beneath the Blast"

Storysouth: "Song of the Compatriots"

Structo: "A Message from the Herd"

Tikkun: "A Different Kind of Person"

Waccamaw: "His Name Means Handsome"

"Harmless Poem" first appeared in *Slate* (April 2008).

"The Passages," "Song of the Drunken Captain," "Standing on Z," and "The Wharves" first appeared in the limited edition chapbook *Standing on Z* (Greensboro: Unicorn Press, 2016).

"When a Child Asks about Angels" first appeared in *The Atlantic* (July/August, 2010).

"Proclamation" first appeared in the pamphlet *Touch Monkey* (Cincinnati: Forklift, Ohio, 2012).

"My Uncle's Sketchbook from the Cold War" first appeared in the Château de Lavigny's twentieth-anniversary anthology (Ledig-Rowohlt Foundation, Switzerland, 2016).

"The Squash Man" first appeared in the anthology *Breaking the Jaws of Silence*, ed. Sholeh Wolpé (Fayetteville: University of Arkansas Press, 2013).

"Evening in the Window, Parts I–IV" appeared in the anthology *The Rag-Picker's Guide to Poetry*, ed. Eleanor Wilner and Maurice Manning (Ann Arbor: University of Michigan Press, 2013).

Children with Enemies

HARMLESS POEM

Forgive the web without its spider,
The houseplant with few or many flowers,
And the stars for hiding in the daytime,
Forgive astronauts for distance
And surgeons for proximity,
Forgive the heart for the way it looks
Like something a dog eats from a pan,
Forgive goat-gods and wine-gods
And the goddess bathing in her pond,
Forgive the sea for being moody,
The air for its turbulence, the stomach
For its vomit, forgive the insistence
Of sperm, the greeting of the ovum,
Forgive orgasms for their intensity
And the faces they make in people's faces,
Forgive the music of liars, forgive autumn
And winter and the departure of lovers.
And the young beautiful dead and the persistence
Of the old, forgive the last tooth and hair.

BECAUSE YOU HAVE SEEN IT SO

Sometimes here in autumn, usually after a rainstorm,
The trees one morning lose their leaves and the light
"Abounds earlie in the newly stripp'd branches"

Through the living room windows. The whole house
Gets exposed inside and out to its angles, the glass
Illuminating all sorts of patterns and prints
"Such the gazer might be delighted by passing clouds."

Certain spiders familiarize themselves with corners,
"Their webs flutter'ng in the breeze of the fire."
Dog fur and dust twine like ivy up the chair legs.

You can tell on the chapped lips of lovers, this winter
Will be long. A child will mourn the death of a houseplant
And draw it in its clay pot with green leaves.
The refrigerator door will keep it among magnets.

A DIFFERENT KIND OF PERSON

I encounter a woman from a long way off
Almost every morning when I walk my dog
In a certain park between certain hours
That have not changed the whole season long.
She owns several coats, all of them
The same length, yesterday a gray one;
Today deep red, and she smoothed her
Cheek as she went by. She sees me
At my worst, unshaven, in my sweats,
Bagging dog shit, my son's skateboard cap
Pulled down to my eyebrows. Hers arch
When she says, "Good morning," which is all
I have ever heard her speak with her accent
From somewhere between the Danube
And the Don, where I bet she modeled coats
In a capital city. How she got here or what
She does is none of my business, and I
Do not wish to say to her more than, "Good
Morning," or ask, "How are you today?"
And spoil the peace we have found among
The ornamental trees native to our region.

THE WHARVES

Rising and falling on the rising tide
The floating docks at dawn sound
Whale songs along the metal posts.

Then the winches and pulleys begin.
There is fog and out to sea a sun
Yet to be seen and cabin lights

Coming on in the pleasure craft
And houseboats moored in the marina
Slips, where bright fenders bump

Against the pilings, lines extending
And slacking, tied to the cleats.
The trawlers are first going out

Against the tide. The largest lead
Ones take the full brunt of the swells,
The others go easy in the wake, while

Overhead gulls follow old bait,
But not all of them are circulating.
Some are fixed to the planks and pilings

Like lampposts. Ashore, two people
Lean against the dockside fence,
Light cigarettes, and drink from a flask.

THE PASSAGES

Some brightly decorated passages,
Lively and fluorescent until dawn,
Like stars are hidden in the daylight—
No signs, no numbers, no names.

Mostly, we live indoors.

I have a favorite pair of shoes
Manufactured in Argentina.
There is nowhere I wish to walk
In them but down those passages.

FRAGMENT

When you consider your own land,
Remote as your childhood room
Where your body grew among
Trophies and pennants to the thing it is
Today,

---

      when you recall the first
Mirror you shaved your face before,
Your image, as a young man,
Weak as it was, appears handsome
From this distance like the city
Where you were born, seen from
The sea past the three-mile limit,

Then rub your body with lotions,
Take pleasure in the wealth of fresh water,
Remember the first time you saw yourself naked.

SONG OF THE COMPATRIOTS

My friend and I are running on a trail
Along the hills outside of town.
I am winded, but he could go for miles,
For hours, for days. He could run
Through the night in the forest and by day
Across the desert along the highway
To Mexico or turn north to the pole.
He could find the land bridge to Asia
And run all the way to the coast of Spain.

We stop in the graveyard above the town.
He says to me, "fatso," though I am thin,
"I want to run for miles, for hours, for days.
I want to run through the night in the forest
And all day across the desert along the highway
To Mexico. I could turn north to the pole
Or find the land bridge to Asia and run
All the way to the coast of Spain,
But not today because you are my friend."

WHEN A CHILD ASKS ABOUT ANGELS

When my brother was swept away in a culvert
During a flash flood and entered a drainpipe
Under a road, the stopped motorists, two elderly
Sisters on their way home from church, counted
Their breath until he spilled out in the ditch
On the other side alive where they cheered him
From the rail and walked down the path in the rain
In their Sunday shoes, flowered hats, and dresses, and they
Guided him through the trees to the shelter of their car.
I am grateful forever to their blanket and thermos
And how they hugged him warm with their bodies
While he was trembling, their huge gorgeous bodies.

THINGS ARE CHANGING FOR JOHANNA

I am a little afraid to walk face-level with the orange cat
Cleaning himself in sunshine on the fence post, so I say

"Hey kitts," to put it on notice I am cool about passing,
When a girl in a calico dress on her knees beside her mom

On the other side of the pickets, weeding the flower bed
And burying bulbs for an upcoming season, gets up

To tell me his name is Reginald but she calls him Reggie.
So I say, "Where it is, Reggie," and he stops washing a minute

And opens his mouth like he's about to answer then decides not to,
Which vexes me a little to think he'd rather lick his rear end

Than regard a fellow who knows something about the world,
When the girl says, "My mom kissed a man on the porch last night,"

And I smile down at her mom wearing overalls and a ball cap
Who is right now the most attractive person in the world.

"THE SUN ON FALLING WATERS WRITES THE TEXT"

I

Once a ray of sunshine broke
Away from the other rays and flew
Across the sky like a banner,

An act of joy.

II

Rapidly moving through a mown field
A goat in high summer
Noticed the bright ray in the sky,

Then snapped at a bee.

III

Woolly woolly,
The beasts of the earth,
The fleas on their bellies

In their own landscape too.

IV

The ray meant nothing to anyone
That did not see it. The ones that saw it
Thought about it endlessly.

I must have slept late that day.

IN THE SEQUENCES OF TRAFFIC

I

Whether I was the doorway leading to the dust-bedazzled entry
Or the warped door leaning in the sunlight against the building
Was the question I asked on the sidewalk and answered both
Ways yes, desiring to trespass in the foyer and ring bells
And talk to people I don't know through their intercoms
Or just slouch awhile against a wall untroubled in the city
Appeared good choices, while through my sunglasses
Occasionally women flipped their hair with the backs of their fingers
In automatic gestures that made me so excited to be alive
I called out to one in a floral dress, "Mademoiselle votre
Cheval est très amusant," and she gave me a look
That strummed once across the strands of my DNA and I
Wanted to wear a t-shirt that said "LET'S SWIM IN THE MUD
TOGETHER" but by then she had joined the greater pattern
Of the avenue in the afternoon where others would encounter her
Waiting for the light to change and think things about the sunlight
On the flowers of her dress and the case they make against death—
And the painters mixed the color and the carpenter returned
From lunch to his recollected bits of song and when I looked
At the door again it was back on its hinges and painted blue.

II

The carpenter returned from lunch to the bits of song
The painters had heard him sing all morning as he planed
The door and sawed and nailed the new boards of the frame
While they painted the walls of the entryway and the hall,
Heard the same four notes they knew of Beethoven's Fifth:
"La dah dah dah," sometimes with words filled in,
Sometimes in English, sometimes in French,
"I love you so," "Elle s'appelle Claire," never getting
Beyond the last note, sometimes pausing several minutes
Or continuing right away, "Tee tee tee tah," notes
That made them wonder when the next might follow
Or whether they might cease forever and be replaced
By the new notes of a new song they would find themselves
Again anticipating, until he sang, "Voilà la porte,"
"Finish your work," and they mixed the blue color
As they traded glances beneath their painter's caps
And looked at their watches and made the best of the hours.

III

After lunch she walked back to the office in the sunshine
Past a carpenter planing a door against a building
And heard the American in dark glasses say something
Silly to her something about her being a funny horse
Which she certainly was not. Last night at the club
She was dancing with friends when a man in a gray shirt
With a fur collar tried to cut in like a man in a cartoon:
Big teeth in his mouth, a long nose, and swirling red circles

In his eyes that made him look as strange as he was.
His breath when he spoke smelled of liquor and meat.
She knew men who carried guns and boys who carried
Knives and knew the men who carried knives and the boys
Who carried guns were the ones to stay away from.
And men with big teeth. She had seen the American before
Talking outside a bar. He was thin and a lot of people knew him.
She would go to that bar and tell him he was the funny horse.
Tonight or another night she would do this.

IV

The afternoon admired itself, pleased by the way it looked
In sunshine on the avenue with so many people outside—
Especially a woman in a spring dress with blue flowers,
And the others—the butcher in front of his shop

Cleaning the glass of the rotisserie, the restaurant
Manager in an apron clipping the leaves off geraniums,
Painters working on the trim of a doorframe, a man in dark glasses
On the corner saying something to the woman in a spring dress

When she passed, a carpenter with his mouth open in such a way
It looked like he was singing, and the cars and buses stopping
And starting. People were looking. People were talking.
The afternoon could not hear them. It was deaf in its weather.

NOTHING ABOUT DOGS

A yellow one and a silver one, both as shaggy
As a sixties bathroom carpet and toilet seat cover,
Sleep under the awning of the porch in a place
They have learned is out of the rain. The yellow one
Looks dirtier because it is lighter but the silver one
Is larger and smells worse, I am told, by a woman
Who appears out of nowhere in her driveway
(Nowhere being outside my field of concentration),
And says the yellow one is on its last legs,
And as if to prove it, it stands on trembling forelegs,
Before flopping down once again on its pal
Like old-time bums in a doorway.
The dust should rise, but the rain tamps it down.
She tells me, her neighbor, their owner,
Has been locked up in the state hospital
For the insane and she looks after them
In case he ever gets out. I recall the story
In the paper. A naked man in his yard fired
A rifle at the sky, but nothing written about dogs.

THE MYSTERIES OF AURORA

I

It is never winter where Aurora lives.
The trees keep their leaves to themselves.
Aurora likes to move through the world with the light
On her face. Like the wife of a president,
She wears a scarf and dark glasses.
But Aurora mourns nothing, not even her childhood.
I don't know whether there are always flowers there.

II

When Aurora says she is an open book
I think of the Kabala and other such texts—
Or my dream of another alphabet
I could not read in which I wrote my work.
Before I knew Aurora I traced petroglyphs
And dinosaur footprints. Now I picture
Her skin covered with invisible symbols.

III

Aurora tries to hide things in bright places
Where she thinks I cannot see them.

Aurora is that kind of magician.
Look over there, she told me,
That cloud looks like my birthmark.
When I turned she was gone,
But I knew which cloud she meant.

IV

When solar particles collide with
The atmosphere Aurora parties till all
Hours of the summer night—Aurora likes
To dance, and I am nasty at the edges
Of the room where young men compose their texts.
Aurora gives out her number but seldom answers.
With Aurora even the echo would be half itself.

V

How unreal, Aurora, a hider in the night,
A personality breeding amid the rookeries
Of stars. Sweet self, how was it
I ever held her, that she held me above
And between saying yeah and oh yeah?
And morning kisses in the garden with coffee.
(A songbird hit the window of the room I wrote this in.)

VI

We walked between the double rows of the plane trees.
I wore the shirt with the pattern she loved. She gave
Herself as only she could. Her auburn hair in highlights newly cut.
Nearly autumn. The leaves in the gutters scuttled in the breeze.
Soon the rails would sing an aubade to the station. Past Aubervilliers,
Flatcars and ridelles idled on the siding. I believe their emptiness
Cheered her for departure with thoughts of their possible cargo.

VII

I live in latitude where the day is brief
And sometimes I sleep through it,
And waking in the middle of the night
I say Aurora is a water glass,
Aurora the pillow, Aurora the blanket.
I think of all the things I have to tell her.
Aurora, the mice who were our witnesses are gone.

CASUALTY EVENT

Amid predictions of the end of the world
And individuals who do their small part
In marketplaces, schools, and airplanes
To turn each other to dust,

I step out of the hospital for a smoke,
And think of the beautiful skin of my father.
His suicide by tile
In the hall he would not carpet

Because it looked so "byoo-tee-ful"
Took nearly three months and a few days into
The New Year. He had heard
Mom call from the other room

When he took his bad step—
And woke only to sing once
To the nurses and offer
Invitations to accompany him abroad.

His skin was
Translucent in the overhead.
His eyes flickered twice
Along with the flat line
Of his ventilated smile.

He is a statue of air now,
And I, both hands in the night,
Pickpocket of sorrow.

MEMORIAL DAY, GREENSBORO

My neighbor loves
This country more
Than the rich do
Because it's all

He's got maybe
Other than his plot
Of earned lawn
Made green with work

And chemicals
His tidy detached
House with someone
Else's family

Initial on
The screen door
(S for Smith?)
A chain link

Fenced yard dog
To patrol amid
Swings and monkey
Bars and his great

Grill flaming
Below traditional
Cuts of meat
He is inside now

Preparing what's next
No one walks
Down the street
It is so quiet

When his air
Conditioner stops
Running the fat
Hisses on the red coals

A greenfly circles
The perimeter
The dog scratches
Its neck and ears

Each flap
Of the flag
Brings us to
Attention

RING OF KEYS

Too many keys on one ring
And most of them open nothing
Anymore. The old suitcases
Lost in the attic eaves
Of the house that poetry
Paid for, the door to the shed
Peeling in the rain, or
To a basement storage unit
In Cambridge twenty years ago
Where I left a mattress
And blanket in case
I might need to crash there.
Here is a long one
To the ignition of my Prelude
And a short, moon-face
To a stolen bike chain.
My locker at the gym
Holds someone's extra
Socks and deodorant,
And this skinny saw blade
From Fort Bliss
Federal Credit Union
Went to a safety deposit box.
(No guns or money there now!)
These toothy ones belong in
The cylinders of my parents'
Apartment in Florida.

They say do not duplicate!
And the last key fits the deadbolt
In the door to my room.
Its millings won't turn
Until I get it just right.

A VISIT TO A STRANGE LAND

Because I could not get my lips around those
Words others spoke like buoyant packages
Along the river of tongues, I could not
Enter the nightly conversations at the inn.
I became all smiles in my responses, trying to
Repeat a successful sound that brought me food,
A greeting that elicited a woman's delight.
The citizens were helpful. They poured my wine
And named the objects laid out on the table
Before me, but I could not get beyond
The walls of their words, and my would-be teachers
Each day grew angrier at my progress
And some felt insulted I had not learned their instructions
And corrected me repeatedly each time
I asked for something to eat. They mocked me
Behind and in front of me and to the side—
One night shouting in my ear saying what
I knew were vulgar phrases, their gestures
Not dissimilar to ones I had been given
In other corners of the world. Then the village
Idiot thumped me hard on the back
And a waitress spilled wine on my lap
And everyone pointed and laughed, till the owner
Stepped out of the kitchen and brought a glass for each
And we joined in a toast I pretended to know.

HIS NAME MEANS HANDSOME

Alvin,
Get the birds going, make sure the sun
Rises out of the sea, keep the tide
Moving, the waves in sets that pause,
Head full of foam, before breaking
On the sandbar, sweep the shadows outside,
Assemble the starfish, sharpen the shells
Of crabs, the teeth of sand sharks, and the fins
Of barracuda, instruct the clouds to be in-
Frequent and thin, the breeze steady and light,
Hold the hours to their schedule, tell
The heat to linger in the pockets of the dunes.
When it falls ask the night what's up.

PROCLAMATION

The governor will give
Homeless people sleeping bags,
Let them stay the night

On windswept porticos
Outside his buildings
Instead of your doorstep.

I am talking to myself
With empty rooms
I cannot bear to live in.

THE BEST FOR ME

Carving out the hard white hearts
After paring the leafy tops, I slice
The berries into my mother's bowl
And hold one reddest of them all,
Shaped like a big toe, plucked
In California who-knows-when,
But here now in the kitchen
I hold it at the instant of its going
From ripe to rotten in my left hand.
Here now, hesitating with the blade
And my own foreknowledge of how
Sweet things can turn out,
I recall she always wanted the best
For me, that I should not trouble myself
Even to make her cereal these odd
Mornings I visit. She sits tired
In the sunshine at the breakfast table.
Tales of evil, death, and misfortune
Spread out before us. Here now I tell her
What I see in the berry. She says,
"Enjoy it yourself." And I do.

WHY POSEIDON CHOSE MY GRANDFATHER

Maybe he needed a suit
Having torn his seaweed raiment—
A three-piece number in brown or green
With pinstripes and wide lapels—

Sort of an old-timey gangster look—
That of the deposed Titan—
Someone you would notice
Getting out of a seahorse limo

Or supping loudly at the raw bar—
So he drowned my grandfather,
A skinny tailor foolish enough
To swim naked in the sea.

OTHERS MADE IT BACK OVER THE PYRENEES

I picture Samuel Bernstein of the Bronx on the night before he left for Spain in my mother's living room saying goodbye to her and my uncles. She gave him the red sweater he tied over his shoulders the day he was killed in action by the Fascists a year later along the banks of the Ebro. "Sammy," she called him, "Sammy," when he held her close at the bottom of the stairs. He sent her five letters when he first got to Madrid. I found them under her stockings in a drawer. "His body's still there," she said when I asked her about him. Then she turned her face in the direction she thought was Spain.

I WAS BUSY

"After living a whole life in a house,
I filled cardboard boxes and tucked their corners,
Marked them, 'Papa's Nightstand,' 'Wedding Dishes,'
'Cabinet over Washing Machine.'

Who has them now?
The fabric of the gray couch
Reminds me of my father's horse.
That straw hat looks like the one it wore
Pulling the wagon to the market in Kovno.

When you live long enough, at the end of your life you get a room
Like this."

MY UNCLE'S SKETCHBOOK
FROM THE COLD WAR

I

It concerned the texture of shadows—
From the corners of the Bahnhof in the summer dawn,
The eeriness of stepping into someone else's day
When that someone has not yet risen, when the soot
Of the night still gauzes the otherwise painted houses
Like a thin dark blanket that covers the body of a person
Asleep amid the wallpaper of a smoker's room.

II

After the forest, the night was brighter in the fields.
He had waved at himself and the shadow of the train
Passing under the light of the constellations.

Here in the capital, the coffee carts had lifted
Their shutters, baked goods arrayed on the counters—
He was hungry and thirsty but afraid to give himself
Away as a foreigner, as if others would not have known
From his shoes or haircut or the manner of his movement
As he carried his suitcase down the stairs of the station
Where others were dispersing in cardinal and ordinal

Directions in the streets around him, while others were
Approaching with various luggage but none as ridiculous
As the one he acquired—composed of pressed wood
And lacquered green and red fabric with brass locks
And a belt he fastened around it to make sure
His paints and brushes would not spill on the sidewalk.

III

He found a hotel where the landlord boiled eggs
And served toast in the morning. A timed light
In the hall at night saw him to his room. What he needed
Were the shadows on the surface of the canal outside
The window and the way the light hid
In the crenellations of the iron bridges he painted
Until the way he saw it among them was no longer of use,
And he felt content to have absorbed the light and no longer
Wanted to paint it. The urge to wander
Stilled like the shadow of a corpse riding on flat water.
He was lonely for his country even if it meant
Painting dams, factories, and electric towers.

IV

Our people are frugal, working the fields
Of our ancestors, plowing the earth with skinny horses,
Wives and daughters tossing seeds from their aprons.

The suitcase beside him like a loyal dog,
His journey to the western cities was over.
He was no longer permitted to travel.
Drinking from bottles in the shadows of a barn,
Men in their undershirts waved not at him
But the length of the train as it passed them.

LITTLE NARCISSUS

While other boys read assigned books
Through thick glasses, I burned insects
With mine and was especially fond of
How centipedes appeared the size of horses
Bucking on fire. My father was
A complicated man and hated that
I did not greet him at the gate
When he came home from his job
Cleaning the river. One evening
In the rain he found me crouching
Under a daffodil tree
And kicked me into a puddle.
Selfish bastard, he screamed
(Others would later)
As my nose broke the surface.
I fought back, Little Narcissus.

A MESSAGE FROM THE HERD

Long ago in the tall grass by sweet waters
We fed and let our young cavort and tarry.
You performed your ceremonies by the river,
And our kind listened to what you call your songs.
You told of the hard times in your story,
When you hung your harps in the willow trees.

Born on your fifth day, we of the field quiver
And twitch. Asleep all night on our hooves,
Our fears are common, our sounds monotonous.
We do not crave the subtleties of your languages:
Words like *cleave* and *hide* and *head*. Or how it is
You pray to rain stones on your neighbor's children.
Lowing in the meadow, no enemies stand grazing.

ANOTHER PICTURE OF THE FUTURE

When the boot lifts
With blood in its tread
Flowers and sunlight
Will be visible above it

And the face of the one
Who wears it will belong
To our neighbor who will rebuild
Our home to give to his children.

THE SQUASH MAN

All these years living in the city, he still was not used to
Walking on concrete. In his province he went barefoot
With his sisters and chased the birds from the fields.
Their father grew squash and was known in the village
As the Squash Man. At ease among the vines,
His grandfather had been the Squash Man too.

All these years living in the city and his feet still hurt him.
When the soldiers took him to war, they gave him boots
That did not fit. After the fields of his province were mined
By the soldiers and the crops rotted on their stalks
And grew moldy where the birds pecked and his mother
Got shot by the soldiers for talking to the rebels and his father
Got shot by the rebels for talking to the soldiers and his sisters
Escaped to the city where the police locked them in a brothel,
He spent his nights searching, his days washing dishes.

His ancestors had always lived on their land.
There was no place else they had known. In the city he slept
Outside in good weather and in abandoned factories in the rainy season.
There were too many streets in the city, too many impasses and alleys.
He would never find his sisters or go back to the countryside.
He would never be the Squash Man. After the soldiers
Planted the mines, some farmers returned to their fields
Because they were starving. A joke went like this:
"What did the farmer say to his neighbor?"
"I would lend you a hand if I had one."

COUPLET ON AN ANCIENT VISAGE

I am the coin struck by the hammer
Whose face made mine crooked forever.

STANDING ON Z

The end of the jetty is like the end of our language.
Nothing is ahead but the open sea.

Who said there should not be more letters in the alphabet?
The jetty would be longer if we spoke Chinese—

But our characters are not as pretty and it takes
Perspective to see how the *m* in *man* and the *w* in *woman*

Suggest the graphics of their respective anatomies.
(Yet in my handwriting one looks like the other.)

I am thinking of the romance of *m* and *w* by the sea.

What do you think they said in the hot sand of creation?
What will their last words be?

ON THE DAY AFTER MY BIRTHDAY

There were gifts I still wanted—
A couch for the porch where I could read,
A camera to take pictures of sunrise
And a certain person before she left me,
A recording I have not heard by Louis Armstrong,
And impossible gifts to receive—
To ride bikes on the boardwalk with Joanne or
Drive around with Joe and Freddie and Bob,
Eat spaghetti in clam sauce at Luigi's or
Sit in the clubhouse at the track with Al,
New books from Bill or Jon or Don or Steve,
Walk to the Square with Mike, play poker with Liam,
And finger the ribbon on the bow of eternity.

MY FAMOUS BROKEN HEART

In my skylit rental
Rain filled the pots and pans.
I went from room to room
Like a poisoned mouse,
Man in pajamas,
Man in slippers,
Man wanting breakfast and
A pretty face at the table.
Bad weather was in the air.
News in sawed-off blasts.
Jackals stitching the periphery
Seized the weakest of the herd.
The temperature dropped.
I stubbed my toe.
The furnace shuddered.
Balloons of my breath
Hung curses in the hall,
And out the window the look
On the trees was not funny
With their ice-coated branches
Or what the night would pull
From its sleeve. Into this
I took my famous broken heart for a walk.

BENEATH THE BLAST

After baiting the mousetrap with bacon fat
And setting it beside the pan where I see nose prints,

Should I take the rodent perspective, following
Crumbs across the countertop in the dark kitchen,

Or choose the voice of the evolved person, hairy
Only in remaining places, forever worrying?

When Jon wrote, "the secret of poetry is cruelty,"
I believe he meant something else that had to do with beauty.

Beauty. Cruelty.
It's the smile of the wire that breaks your neck.

QUESTIONS FOR THE MARINER

How could you forget the sea
If only for a moment, forget the waves,
The gulls, the drawings in the sand,
Forget the currents beyond the breakers,
Forget seaweed and dolphins and squid,
How could you forget sharks or whales,
Improbable swordfish and sunken ships?

Did you forget how our Earth, like your body,
Contains mostly water and that you
Are a creature swimming through the world
With your own sea inside you?

46

ATTIC AND BASEMENT

When she said I had no room
For her in my life, all I saw when I closed
The phone was emptiness stretched out
Like the earth beneath my house,

And unlike her body those words never
Left me, like snow affixed to the roof
Of the world I had forgotten while
Living as I do so close to the ground.

OKAY TO OTHERS

It is dangerous to make such requests,
But I will tell you my day since you asked. I rose
Early and walked the dog while the children were
Sleeping and tried to keep them safe in my thoughts even
Though I was only going around the block, not back
To Paris or New York or coming to Atlanta. And while
I walked I tried not to think of her, the one you said
Not to fall for again but did. And I was talking
To myself again out loud but since the dog was with me
I looked okay to others. I tried to think of my work and what
I would do later when the children went back to their mother.
And already it was almost four in the afternoon when
You texted *how annoying lovers can be,*
Meaning yours and knowing how it was going with mine.
You should be afraid that I am older and have not learned
Not to drive through the night for a kiss.

FUTURE GIRL

She found the draft of his poem concerning Future Girl
On the back of an envelope he had left by the keyboard.

It began, "Even as I was begging the woman I loved not to go,
I had already been in touch with Future Girl.

Future Girl with her cape and antennae.
Future Girl with her emblem shirt and tight-fitting hose.

Future Girl who would take me from my past ..."
It was all he had and too much.

WITHOUT SUNGLASSES

An invisible dog
Makes me a blind man
This morning being pulled
Down the avenue where the sun
Fills my eyes with gold.

Where am I going, Big Fella,
Without my sunglasses on a day
I really need them? Too early,
Too harsh, too sudden, too shiny
The pavements of my city,

The walls of graffiti
Gaudy as Byzantium.
I wait for the light to change.
No one at the intersection.

WHAT BEGINS IN EROS ENDS IN ELEGY

Waiting for the phone to ring like a held-back orgasm,
I hesitate in position between the clock and the show

On television where a man sleeps in the carcass
Of a camel to keep warm in the desert at night—

I try to write and my dead teacher's words come back.
Say distance, he told me, when you mean silence.

EVENING IN THE WINDOW (PARTS I–IV)

I

She and he sit in the open window and if you saw them
You would say that most everything is white around them—
The painted walls, the high ceiling, the open curtain
Whose blue and green flowers are pressed between the folded
Pleats, and most of all the white stone buildings like the one
Across the narrow street where things have always happened.
It is a double window in the French style but of modern
Design. One floor up from the pavement, she and he
Drink and smoke: he keeping his weight on his feet as he leans
On the sill; she perching, her back against the right
Frame; both taking their places each evening though
Neither needs to say it, as in the way they silently chose
Who made the first touch, what side of the new bed
To take as their own. And if you saw them that evening
In the window just as it was closing, when the white
Of the sky matched the white of the stone and the white
Curtain through the light revealed its bright pattern in
The moment after their fingers hinged and released, you'd think
They were not parting but removing what was left between them.

II

He walked past the window and if you were watching you
Would know they were no longer there since that evening, their last
Together when they drank and smoked and talked about themselves
And watched the narrow street that was their street for a time
When they still could talk about what they had left between them.
The glass was black as the street and the sky as absent of light
As the room behind the drawn curtains in their frames where
He pictured the twin beds they had pushed together, her clothes
Scattered to be packed, and the last image of their bodies glazed
In the mirror, when she had said, "Look." It was no longer their season
She told him later, as if she were speaking of the pitted fruit of summer—
But true enough the heat of the city was gone and the stone buildings
That had absorbed it were cold in the dark. He never had been in this
City in winter before, never had felt the wind this way off the river
Through the elevated and narrow streets, could not keep from coming back
To the one beneath their window where they had leaned together—
Where they had drunk and smoked and talked in summer and closed
The window and taken off their clothes and parted the next morning
At the station by the ruins. Had you seen him again you would know them.

III

She stood alone in the window of a fine hotel room
In the city she last saw when he was the same age she had
Become. His spirit filled the empty place beside her on the sill
Just as she knew this would happen when she returned
To this city where she and he once stood in the window
Of the apartment they had rented in a nearby quarter
Where they drank and smoked and talked about everything
But their future. She was twice as old now as she was that summer.
Jet-lagged a little, lying in bed after dinner, she had forgotten
How long it stayed light out. She pictured their last evening
In the window together, how it was they were with each other,
The bedspread and top sheet pushed to either side of them
Like curtains, the plaster ceiling like the wall of the building
Across the street from the apartment they had taken
Near the ruins where they did not have to be secret
(You might have seen them), where they closed the window
That last evening together, a black and white series she would paint later
Across the threads of a canvas: a man's arms around the blurred figure
Of a woman in motion at the edge of the bed to what waited beyond them.

IV

The years gone by did not treat the city well and the age
It slipped into was like those it had endured in the past.
Its government fell. Once more its own citizens
Set public buildings on fire. Occupying armies
Awaited treaties inside the former gates. The black soot
Cleaned from the structures a century before built up again,
And the walls of the building across the street from the window
Where he and she talked and smoked in the evening
That summer had long darkened into shadow. You might say
The weather had altered with the city's fortunes.
The river froze in winter and colonies of rats grew fearless.
There were sieges and shortages and power failures.
Graves were looted and zoo animals slaughtered.
The frame where she and he once sat and talked in the window
And drank and smoked was now sealed with bricks the last
Residents loosened from the pavement and with stones quarried
From the ruins. The quarter was empty but not as it was
The August of their inhabitation when others were merely traveling.
Whoever you are, whatever you saw, what is it you still ask from them?

SONG OF THE DRUNKEN CAPTAIN

The cables in the marina cut
The horizon into several lines
And the docks at this angle

Divide the bay. Like the joke
About the boat being a hole
In the water you pour money into,

Last night I poured too much
Liquor into my throat. Now
In my bunk as the sun comes up,

I look through the port-
Hole just above the waterline
Into a day I do not wish

To sail into, I hear the mates
With their singing voices
Shouting to the pilot boat

To throw them the lines.
They will take their cargo
O all the way to Jakarta.

IF I HAD KNOWN YOU WERE LISTENING

I would have told you about the ice cave,
How the storm on the glacier sent me
Where others and animals had been.

I would have told you about the ice cave
That stank in the thin dark air
Where others and animals had been.
Even though their bodies were frozen,

They stank in the thin dark air,
And I could not breathe inside
Even though the bodies were frozen
And I had my bottled oxygen

And I could not breathe inside
And I camped out on the mountain
And I had my bottled oxygen
And the wind left no prints on the snow.

THE LIVES OF MY FRIENDS

The sun may be bright but it is not clear
To me why I feel as I do, feeling my way

Along the shadowy sidewalks that show
No traces of the footprints that should

Have worn the concrete down to earth,
No hard evidence of the lives of my friends

Or scrap of fabric upon a random thorn;
Their jackets, coats, and winter wraps

Boxed or tossed or sold to vintage shops
With shirts and pants and summer frocks;

Their ties and scarves and woolen hats
Gone to build the wings of moths;

They loved to let their rooms grow dark.
And when they died they gave away their hearts.

TRANSLATION FROM THE ORIGINS OF TIME

Dawn and Dusk live down the block and up the street.
They have worked different shifts since the origins
Of time—even before the winds calmed
And Night and Day were born.

But never could Dawn seek Dusk's comfort.
But never did Dusk blaze in Dawn's glory.
Night and Day are long to me now.
My parents are gone for whom I was the world.

NOTES

"Song of the Compatriots" is for Michael Parker. "Song of the Drunken Captain" is for Revell Carr.

"The sun on falling waters writes the text" is a line from Gerard Manley Hopkins's poem "It was a hard thing to undo this knot."

"If I Had Known You Were Listening" loosely concerns Dudley Wolfe, who died climbing K2 in 1939.

My gratitude, always, to Thomas Lux.